ESL Games for Teens & Adults:

No Prep ESL Games for the Classroom. Perfect Teaching Materials for TEFL Lesson Plans (Games, Warmers & Fillers)

Copyright © 2019 **Marc Roche**

Copyright © 2019 by Marc Roche. All Rights Reserved.

No part of this ESL Games publication may be reproduced, distributed, or transmitted in any form or by any means, including photocopying, recording, or other electronic or mechanical methods, or by any information storage and retrieval system without the prior written permission of the publisher, except in the case of very brief quotations embodied in critical reviews and certain other noncommercial uses permitted by copyright law.

Topics Covered in this ESL Games book:

ESL Games, esl games for the classroom, esl games for adults, esl books for adults, esl books for adults advanced, esl conversation books for adults, esl books, esl books for teachers, ESL speaking games, Business English speaking lessons, Business English speaking activities, ESL speaking activities, ESL speaking books, ESL conversation, ESL lesson plans, ESL conversation cards, business English conversation books for adults.

Roche Pub ESL Books. All rights reserved

Sign up for exclusive resources + free e-books + tons of other resources and goodies at the end of the book

Copyright © 2019 **Marc Roche**

Contents

Get Marc Roche's Starter Library FOR FREE 10

About This ESL Games Book 11

About the Author 12

Other Books By Marc Roche 13

SECTION 1: ESL GAMES FOR ADULTS & TEENS 14

    Pictionary / Charades 15

    Hangman 17

    Tic Tac Toe 18

    Toilet Paper Squares 19

    Think Fast 20

    Words at Sea 21

    Easy Anagrams 24

    What Do They Look Like? 25

    Sentence Race 27

    Getting to Know You 29

    Alphabet Stop 31

    Role Play 33

    Twenty Questions 35

    Forbidden Words 37

    Truth or Lie? 39

    Good Advice 41

    When I'm Head Teacher 43

    Storytelling 45

A Day in the Life of an Animal 48
SECTION 2: ADULT/ BUSINESS CONVERSATION QUESTIONS 50
1. WORK 51
2. DAYS OFF 52
3. AGE AT WORK 53
4. JOB LOCATION 54
5. WORKING FROM HOME 55
6. OFFICE LOCATION 56
7. WORKING OVERSEAS 58
8. OFFICE LUNCH 59
9. AFTER WORK ACTIVITIES 60
10. REWARDS AND RECOGNITION 61
11. TEAM BUILDING 62
12. OFFICE SUPPLIES AND EQUIPMENT 63
13. WORKING HOURS 64
14. OVERTIME 65
15. BUSINESS TRIPS 66
16. EXPERIENCE 67
17. PROMOTION & DEMOTION 68
18. PROBATIONARY PERIOD: 69
19. CONTRACTS 70
20. WORK-LIFE BALANCE 72
21. MANAGEMENT & LEADERSHIP 74

22. BEING AN EMPLOYEE 76
23. FREELANCING 77
24. DIFFERENT PROFESSIONS 78
25. JOB REQUIREMENTS 80
26. JOB INTERVIEWS 81
27. BENEFITS & PERKS 83
28. RESIGNATION 84
29. JOB-HOPPING 85
30. SALARY 86
31. CHOOSING A COMPANY 87
32. FEELINGS ABOUT YOUR JOB 88
33. OFFICEMATES/CO-WORKERS 89
34. RETIREMENT 90
35. EMAIL 91
36. MEETINGS 92
37. CONFERENCES 93
38. TECHNOLOGY 94
39. OFFICE ENVIRONMENT 95
** BONUS SPEAKING CARDS SECTION ** 96
40. MEDIA 97
41. HOTELS 99
42. LANGUAGES 101
43. TECHNOLOGY 103
44. ART 105

45. HISTORY	107
46. BOOKS	109
Speaking Phrases (Student Handout)	111
Sign up to my newsletter for a Free Book and TONS of FREE Resources & Goodies!	114
One Last Thing…	115

Get Marc Roche's Starter Library for Free

Sign up for the no-spam newsletter and get an introductory book and lots more exclusive content, all for free.

Details can be found at the end of the book.

About this ESL Games Book

These ESL games and instant conversation worksheets can be adapted to suit any level, objective and age as warmers, introductions, review activities or fillers to provide language practice and opportunities for feedback. They have been tried and tested in ESL classrooms all over the world with great success.

Whether you're teaching children, teens or adults, knowing some good classroom activities is a must for any TESOL teacher. However interesting your lessons are, there will always be a point where students get bored of writing and listening - so having something prepared which will get them talking, laughing and even moving around will help them to stay engaged. Informal exercises are also an important way to get students comfortable with speaking and listening, and can help to put vocabulary and grammar into a practical context.

While planned activities are important, it's also always worth having a few quick and easy games in mind in case you have time left over at the end of a lesson - so from quick games to creative projects, here are some of the best activities suitable for students at every level.

About the Author

Marc is originally from Manchester and currently lives in Malaga, Spain. He is a writer, teacher, trainer, writer and business manager. He has collaborated with organizations such as the British Council, the Royal Melbourne Institute of Technology and University of Technology Sydney among others. Marc has also worked with multinationals such as Nike, GlaxoSmithKline or Bolsas y Mercados. Marc is also an avid learner and has carried out extensive research in various fields ranging from business leadership to marketing and neuroscience. In his free time, he likes to travel, cook, write, play sports, watch football (Manchester City and Real Madrid) and spend time with friends and family.

Learn more about Marc at amazon.com/author/marcroche

Learn more about Marc's Training Company at https://www.idmadrid.es/

OTHER BOOKS BY MARC ROCHE

IELTS WRITING: ADVANCED WRITING MASTERCLASS (IELTS TASKS 1 & 2): IELTS ACADEMIC WRITING BOOK BAND 7.0 - 8.5

TOEFL Writing Simple: Advanced Writing Course for TOEFL Tasks 1 & 2

101 Grammar Rules for IELTS: Instant Study Notes (IELTS Grammar)

Legal English: Contract Law: Basic to Advanced TOLES (Legal English and TOLES Preparation Book 1)

SECTION 1: ESL GAMES FOR ADULTS & TEENS

Pictionary / Charades

Level: Any

Good for: Vocabulary review / Quick end of lesson activities

Preparation:

Write out a list of familiar or recently-learned vocabulary on to pieces of paper - topics like professions, weather, food, actions, sports and animals are always good.

Split the class into two teams.

Activity:

Teams take it in turns to send student up to the whiteboard, where they are given a paper with one of the words on it. They then have 30 seconds to draw a picture of what they've read, while the rest of their team guesses what it is.

Rules:

If a team guesses the word in time, they get a point. The first team to set number of points wins.

You can also play this game with actions rather than drawings - so the student has to mime the word without speaking, writing, or making any sound.

Hangman

Level: Any

Good for: Spelling review / Quick end of lesson activities

Preparation:

Divide the class into two teams and choose a word from recently learned vocabulary. Draw out a hangman game on the board.

Activity:

The teams take it in turns to guess a letter. Correct letters go into their blank spaces, while wrong guesses add a new part to the hanged man.

Rules:

The teams take it in turns until one guesses the word correctly and wins a point - in later rounds, you can also allow a student to choose the word for their opposing team to guess.

If all of the parts of the hanged man are drawn before a team can guess the word, no points are given.

Tic Tac Toe

Level: Any

Good for: Vocabulary review / End of lesson activities

Preparation:

Split the class into two teams and draw a tic tac toe grid on the board, with the squares numbered one to nine. Prepare up to 20 review questions or picture cards.

Activity:

Teams take it in turns to choose a number from the square of their choice. They are then asked the corresponding question or shown the picture card. If they correctly name the picture or get the question right, they can claim the square - if they get it wrong, the square remains free, and the other team can claim it by answering a different question correctly.

Rules:

The goal is for one team to claim three squares in a line - either vertically, diagonally, or horizontally.

Toilet Paper Squares

Level: Any

Good for: Icebreakers

Preparation:

A toilet paper roll is passed around the classroom, and every student takes at least three squares.

Activity:

Once everyone has taken some, they have to count how many squares they have, and then tell the class one fact about themselves for each square of toilet paper they are holding - in English, of course! The activity of handing around the toilet roll, especially when students don't know the rules of the game, is a great way to get everyone focused and excited at the start of a new term.

If students are struggling to come up with statements, do some practice as a group, reviewing good examples. Complexity can vary depending on the level of the class.

Think Fast

Level: Any

Good for: Vocabulary review / End of lesson Activities

Preparation:

Announce a topic for vocabulary review and choose one student to keep time and another to count how many correct answers are given. Then choose three to five students to leave the classroom and wait outside.

Activity:

Ask one of the students to come back into the classroom. They then have 20 seconds to list as many words as they can on the chosen topic. Once they're finished, invite in the next student, and so on. The one who comes up with the most words wins - repetition and made up words don't count!

Rules:

You can play as many rounds as you like, choosing a new topic and selecting new students each time. It's also helpful to invite the rest of the class to name any words they think the other students missed at the end of each round.

Words at Sea

Level: Any

Good for: Vocabulary review / Longer Activities

Preparation:

Students form groups of four or five - each group being one Ship. They then need to choose a Ship name - encourage them to think of animals, colors, countries, or movie stars that they like.

Each group then has to elect a Shooter and a Captain. The Captain's job is to remember the name of their own Ship. They will have to answer if another team calls out their name. The Shooter has to remember the name of the other Ships in the classroom.

Once the teams are formed, all of the Captains form a circle, with their other crew members in a line behind them, and the Shooter at the back.

Next, tell the students the topic of the vocabulary review - this can be anything from items of clothing to irregular verbs depending on the ability level of the class. The game works best when the subject matter has a lot of vocabulary for students to choose from.

Each Ship then has two minutes to think of as many words as possible and memorize them.

Activity:

Choose a team to start and call out their Ship's name. The Captain of the ship must then say one of the words from the chosen topic. For example, if the topic is items of clothing, they might say 'SCARF'. The student next in line behind the Captain then says another word, such as 'SHIRT', and the person behind them does the same - and so on until they reach the Shooter.

Rather than saying another vocabulary word, the Shooter instead chooses another Ship, and calls out their name. That Ship then has to do exactly the same thing - working back from the Captain from the Shooter.

Rules:

Shooters can't name their own Ship or choose one that's already been called.

Words can't be repeated, and everyone has to come up with a new word within three seconds. If a group takes too long, can't think of a new word or repeats one, or if a Shooter calls the name of a Ship that has already has a turn, their Ship has 'sunk'

When a Ship sinks, its crew (including the Captain and Shooter) goes to join another one.

Once every Ship has had a turn, the round is over. For the next round, choose another topic and carry on -, with the groups getting bigger as more Ships sink. The last Ship that hasn't sunk is the winner.

Easy Anagrams

Level: Easy / Medium

Good for: Spelling review / Quick end of lesson activities

Preparation:

Write out a jumble of nine letters on the board - for example H F O H R K S T I. Make sure there is a mix of vowels and consonants. You can prepare the letters in advance if you want to include specific vocabulary.

Activity:

Give students 30 seconds to write down as many words as they can make out of the nine letters. So, in this case, they might list 'hit', 'shirt', 'skirt', 'fork', and so on.

Rules:

Words must all be in English and spelled correctly! The student with the most words is the winner.

What Do They Look Like?

Level: Easy / Medium

Good for: End of lesson activities

Preparation:

Every student is given a piece of paper, and one is selected to go first.

Activity:

The selected student starts describing a person without using their name, and all of the other students draw them on their paper. Once the description is finished, the students share their drawings.

Rules:

The person can be real - a celebrity or fictional character - or completely made up, although it's more fun if it's someone that everyone knows.

The game can be adapted to be about animals - or can be used to encourage students to draw a 'monster' by coming up with fantastical descriptions. It can also be used to practice questions and answers - by inviting students to ask questions about what the person or animal looks like.

Sentence Race

Level: Easy / Medium

Good for: Vocabulary review

Preparation:

Choose an area of vocabulary to review and write out a selection of words on small pieces of paper. For this game, the class will be split into two teams, and each will be given an identical set of words - so make two copies of every word and make them into two identical piles. To ensure that everyone can take part, make sure you have enough words for the whole class to play - and don't forget to keep a record of the words for yourself as well!

Activity:

Divide the class into two teams and invite them to come up with team names. Give both teams an identical bundle of papers and get them to share them out until every student has one piece of paper with a review word on it.

Call out one of the vocabulary words. One student from each team should have that word on their piece of paper. They then run to the whiteboard and write a sentence containing that word.

Rules:

The fastest student is the winner - however, if a sentence isn't readable, doesn't make sense, or isn't spelled correctly, they are disqualified.

Getting to Know You

Level: Easy / Medium

Good for: Icebreakers / Conversation practice

Preparation:

Give each student a piece of paper and split them into teams of two. Before starting, review some 'getting to know you' questions - for example, 'How many brothers and sisters do you have?', 'What subject do you like best and why?', or 'What's your favorite movie'. Questions can be more or less complex depending on the ability level of the class.

Activity:

In their pairs, students ask each other five or six questions. They can note down their partner's answers on their paper if they like. Both people should have the chance to answer.

After everyone has finished, all of the students change partners, and tell their new partner about the person they just spoke to, using the information they just learned.

Once everyone has shared with their second partner, students stand up one by one and tell the rest of the class about the student they just learned about.

To make this game more listening-focused, you can take away the papers - so students only pass on what they remember. In this version, you can also get the rest of the class to guess who a student is describing at the end.

ALPHABET STOP

Level: Easy / Medium

Good for: Vocabulary Review / Big Classes

Preparation:

Give each student a piece of paper with category names across the top or get them to make their own (though this may take time). The categories can be customized to suit the vocabulary you've studied, but options such as Places, Animals, Activities, Objects, Fruit and Vegetables, Clothes etc. all work well. There should also be a Total column at the end.

Activity:

One student starts saying the alphabet out loud, from A to Z, until you shout 'STOP' at a random letter.

All of the students then have to write a word in each category, starting with that letter. So, if it was 'L', they might write Los Angeles, Llama, Listening, Lightbulb, Lemon and Leggings.

Rules:

The first student to write a word in every column shout 'STOP!' and everyone has to put their pens down.

Students then exchange their sheets, and everyone shares the words they chose. Write a list of them on the board - at the end, any words that were added by more than three students are worth 10 points. Words that were only chosen by two students get 20 points. Words that only one person picked get 50 points. Of course, all words have to be spelled correctly and fit in their category!

Students then add up their neighbor's points, and the one with the most wins the round.

This game can alternatively be played with a timer - so students have one or two minutes to put as many words as they can in every category. In this version there are no points - the student with the most correct words wins.

ROLE PLAY

Level: Easy / Medium

Good for: Conversation practice

Preparation:

Start off by talking about vocabulary you've recently studied. Ask students who they think would use it, and why. For example, if they have been learning about weather, it might be people who are going on holiday, or who want to do an outdoor activity. Think about what other questions might be part of the same conversation - for example, what clothes you should wear.

Get two students to read out a prep-prepared sample conversation between two people on a relevant topic - for example:

TOM

Where are you going on holiday?

MARY

I'm going to Thailand.

TOM

What is the weather like there?

MARY

It's very hot and sunny, and it rains a lot in monsoon season.

TOM

You'll need to take an umbrella!

Then split the class into pairs.

Activity:

Instruct the pairs to each write a new conversation using your reviewed vocabulary. For more advanced students, you can set a minimum number of lines or ask them to incorporate multiple topics.

Then choose some of the students to perform their conversations to the rest of the class.

Twenty Questions

Level: Medium

Good for: Conversation practice / End of lesson activity

Preparation:

Make sure to go over question and answer formats with the class before starting.

Activity:

Choose an item or activity, then go around the class inviting students to ask yes or no questions to try and guess what it is - such as 'is it heavy?', 'does it make a sound?', 'do you do it at school?'', or 'is it fun?'. They are allowed to ask a maximum of 20 questions, plus three guesses at the end.

Rules:

The first student to correctly guess the item or action gets to choose the next word and answer questions from the rest of the class.

This game can also be played by splitting the class into pairs - with one person in every pair choosing the word, and the other asking the questions. If doing it this way, give them around five minutes to play one round, then switch. For lower ability classes, it can be helpful to provide the students with papers or cards containing words or pictures suitable for the game, so they don't have to choose their own.

Forbidden Words

Level: Medium / Difficult

Good for: Vocabulary review

The activity is a simplified version of the popular game Taboo.

Preparation:

Make a series of cards, each containing one word written in large letters, with a circle around it. Below that word are also written between two and four related words, written in smaller letters - these are the forbidden words.

Put one chair at the front of the room, facing towards the board. Place one to three other chairs opposite it, facing away from the board - depending on how many students are in each team.

Split the class into teams of two to four and make a table on the board to keep track of points.

Activity:

The first team comes up and sits in the chairs at the front of the class - one student is designated the role of explainer, and they sit in the chair facing the board. Their teammates are guessers, and they face away from the board. The aim of the game is for the explainer to help their teammates work what the word inside the circle is, by describing it without saying any of the forbidden words.

Once the first team has successfully guessed the word or given up, a new team comes to the front and new words are written on the board. When every team has had a go, the first team can come up again - but with a different student taking the role of explainer.

Rules:

If any of the forbidden words are used, the team gets zero points! The team with the most points wins. You can also put a time limit on describing and guessing the word (one minute is usually enough) to make things more exciting.

Truth or Lie?

Level: Medium / Difficult

Good for: Big classes / Icebreakers / older students

Preparation:

Divide the class into groups of two to four students and give everyone a piece of paper with five questions on it - each person in a group should have different questions.

Questions should be focused around experiences, and start 'Have you ever' - for example, have you ever met someone famous? / been on the news? / danced in public? / won a medal?

Activity:

One student (A) in each group goes first, and answers one of the questions from their teammates' lists. No matter whether they have done the activity or not, they have to answer, 'Yes I have'. The other people in the group then have to ask five more questions (in any format this time) to determine whether or not student A is telling the truth - for example 'when did you do it?', 'who were you with?', or 'did you get into trouble?'

Student A's goal is to convince their teammates that they really have done what's on the card. If they haven't done it, they'll need to make up answers to the follow-up questions and trying to be as convincing as possible.

After five follow-up questions, student A secretly writes down whether the question was true or false, while their teammates write down their guess. The game then moves on, with a new teammate taking the role of student A and answering a new question.

Rules:

After everyone has answered three or more questions (depending on how much time is available), the students reveal their answers to each other. The most convincing liar wins!

Good Advice

Level: Medium / Difficult

Good for: Creative thinking

Preparation:

Come up with a list of problems and goals. They can be real or imaginative - from 'I am always late for class' and 'I keep losing my keys' through to 'I want to have a pet lion' or 'I wish I was rich'.

Activity:

Pick a question and write it on the board or read it out loud. Then go around the class, inviting students to give you advice on how you can solve your problem or reach your goal. Encourage creative and silly answers.

After going through a few questions, choose a student to stand up and come up with a problem or a goal of their own, again inviting the other students to suggest solutions.

If the class are struggling to get started, try going through some examples together. It's also worth reviewing correct sentence structure for answers - practicing 'I think', 'you should', 'you could try' and so on.

WHEN I'M HEAD TEACHER

Level: Difficult

Good for: Writing practice / Group activity / Full lesson

Preparation:

Write the premise on the board and explain it to the class -

'You are now the Head Teacher of this school! You have two years to make the school perfect. You can spend as much money as you want, but everything has to be finished in two years. What will you do?'

Discuss the kinds of things students might want to think about - What changes would they make straight away, and which ones would take longer? What would they do to make it better for students, and what would they do for teachers? What would make them happier, healthier, better at studying? If students are struggling, you can put some prompts on the board, such as buildings, sports, free time, library, teachers, food, music, curriculum, schedule, etc.

Encourage them to be as specific as possible - so rather than just saying 'We should have better lunches', they should talk about what food would be on their perfect menu. It's also important to remind the students that they are the headteacher in this scenario! So, cancelling all the classes wouldn't work out very well.

Activity:

Give the class 15 minutes to work individually on their answers, writing down their thoughts (they only need to write notes for their own use in this activity - so let them know their writing won't be marked). Then put them into groups of three to five and give them the rest of the lesson to share ideas within their groups and put together presentations that they will give to the class next lesson, explaining what their perfect school would look like. It can be helpful for each group to have a leader, to lead the presentation and help the group to organize their ideas.

Next lesson give the groups ten minutes to practice. They then take it in turns to deliver their presentations - with time for questions and answers at the end of each one. At the end of the final presentation, students vote on which idea of the perfect school they like best.

This activity can also be adapted to different topics - for example, the perfect town, city or country.

Storytelling

Level: Difficult

Good for: Creative writing

Preparation:

Bring a pack of cards, and a list of 13 adjectives that could describe the action in a story - one for each type of card. For example:

A - Fun

2 - Frightening

3 - Sad

4 - Romantic

5 - Crazy

6 - Exciting

7 – Heart-breaking

8 - Dramatic

9 - Unexpected

10 - Fantastic

J - Weird

Q - Tense

K - Dangerous

You will also need a theme for the story - something like 'Your teacher goes on vacation' or 'A girl learns magic' - choose a topic that the class will engage with, and/or which relates to recent areas of study.

Activity:

Start off by telling the beginning of the story - then hand it over to the class. Choose a student to draw one card from the pack. The number on the card will decide what type of thing will happen next. For example, it they take a 4, something romantic must happen - such as two characters falling in love, a new love interest entering the story, or someone going to a wedding.

Let students contribute their ideas by raising their hands and continue the story together. If two good suggestions are made, let the class vote on their favorite. Keep telling the story until all of the cards have been drawn - you can reduce the deck to just two suits if you have limited time.

The story must end by the end of the deck, so encourage students to wrap things up when you get down to the final cards. At the end, discuss your favorite moments together.

For more advanced students focusing on creative writing, this activity can also be done by getting students to write down their stories individually, and then sharing them at the end or in the next lesson.

A Day in the Life of an Animal

Level: Difficult

Good for: Discussion / Creative writing

Preparation:

Ask students to think of an answer to the question 'if you could be any animal for a day, what would it be?'. Encourage them to explore fewer common options by providing them with a list of possible creatures, or by having a brief discussion first.

Activity:

Ask students to think about what a day as their chosen animal would be like. What would they do, and where would they be? How did they get there? What would they be excited about? What would they be afraid of?

Give them five minutes to write down a few sentences, using the voice of their animal - for example 'I am an arctic fox living on a glacier. It's cold, and I'm afraid that I won't find enough food to eat. I have four cubs at home, and they are hungry'.

Get the students to share their stories, then ask them to think about why they chose their animal.

Next, tell them to think about what a day in the life of their animal would be like if the animal was in captivity, and write new sentences with that in mind. You can explore other ideas here as well - for example, if they couldn't live in their home any more, or if their species was endangered.

If focusing on creative writing, encourage them to look at the differences between their first ideas and their new ones - discuss how putting a character into a new situation can change who they are and what motivates them.

Alternatively, for a discussion-focused lesson, use the topic as a launchpad for discussing subjects from global warming and hunting to the things that they appreciate in their own lives.

SECTION 2: ADULT/ BUSINESS CONVERSATION QUESTIONS

These instant conversation worksheets can be adapted into games, such as board games and other classroom activities to provide speaking practice and opportunities for feedback.

The teacher can also use them with a timer if he or she wants to add some pressure to the activity, to make the activity more exciting or to prepare students for an exam such as Cambridge Business, where time is a factor. For example: students can work in pairs and speak for 1 to 2 minutes about each question as a mini-presentation type activity. Their partner can keep the time and provide feedback, while the teacher circulates the classroom and helps different pairs of students.

1. WORK

What do you do?

What does your job position entail?

Can you describe your tasks on a daily basis?

What is your favorite task at work?

What is your least favorite task at work?

How would you describe your current job?

2. DAYS OFF

How many days do you work in a week?

How many hours do you work in a day?

How many days do you work in a year?

How many vacation leaves do you have?

How many sick leaves do you have?

How many days off do you have in a week?

How many days off do you have in a month?

What do you do during your day off?

What do you do during your vacation leave?

3. AGE AT WORK

At what age did you start working?

What is the ideal age for someone to start working?

What is the ideal age for someone to stop working?

At what age would you want to retire?

At what age do people start working in your country?

At what age do people retire in your country?

4. JOB LOCATION

What jobs are available in your hometown?

What will make you consider working in your hometown?

Why did you choose to work in your hometown?

What jobs are available in your city?

What will make you consider working in the city?

Why did you choose to work in the city?

What is the most popular city in your country in terms of job hunting?

What is the most sought-after business center in your country?

What is the ideal city for you to work in?

5. WORKING FROM HOME

In your own words, how would you define working from home?

What is a good excuse to work from home?

How do you stay productive working from home?

What are the benefits of working from home?

What are the disadvantages of working from home?

What would it take for you to permanently work from home?

How popular are work from home jobs in your country?

Should working from home be an option for all office workers?

6. OFFICE LOCATION

How far do you live from your office?

How many hours do you commute in total per week?

What mode of transportation do you use to get to work?

How much time do you spend in traffic?

How much do you spend on transportation?

Would you consider renting an apartment near your office?

How far is your office from the nearest mall?

How far is your office from the nearest park?

How far is your office from the nearest hang out place?

How far is your office from the nearest train station?

How far is your office from the nearest bus stop?

How many floors does your work building have?

7. WORKING OVERSEAS

How would you consider working overseas?

In your opinion/experience, what is the best country to work in?

In your opinion/experience, what is the worst country to work in?

If you were given a chance, which country would you like to work in?

What would you consider before working overseas?

Why do some people prefer to work abroad?

What type of people are ideal for working overseas?

What type of people do you think would not be successful working overseas?

8. OFFICE LUNCH

Where do you usually eat out during lunch break?

How often do you usually take for your lunch break?

Who do you eat out with at work?

When do you usually eat out at work?

How much do you usually spend when you eat out at work?

What do you usually order when you eat out at work?

Why do people prefer eating out than eating in the office?

Why do some people prefer eating home cooked meals in the office than eating out?

9. AFTER WORK ACTIVITIES

Where do you usually hang out after work?

How often do you usually hang out after work?

Who do you hang out with after work?

How much do you usually spend when you hang out with your co-workers?

How far is the nearest place where you can hang out?

Why do so many people hangout after work?

Why do many people choose not to hangout after work?

In your country, what is the most common hangout activity after work?

10. REWARDS AND RECOGNITION

Why should employers recognize employees' efforts?

How are employees recognized for their achievements in your office?

How should an employer recognize an employee?

When was the last time an employee was recognized in your office?

When was the last time you were recognized at work?

How would you feel if you were recognized for the quality of your work? What reward would you like to receive?

11. TEAM BUILDING

Why is it important to have team building activities? Who benefits the most in team building, employees or employers?

When was the last time you participated in a team building activity?

What is the best team building activity in your opinion?

What is your least favorite team building activity?

How does team building help a business/company?

Who should choose the venue of the team building exercises? Why?

Who should choose the activities of the team building exercises? Why?

12. OFFICE SUPPLIES AND EQUIPMENT

What office supplies do you have at your desk?

What office supplies do you often use?

What office supplies do you seldom use?

What office supplies would you like to be available in your company?

13. WORKING HOURS

What do you think about 9 to 5 jobs? Would you prefer a different time-table? Why?

In your opinion, how many hours should someone work in a day? Why?

In your opinion, how many days should someone work in a week? Why?

14. OVERTIME

When was the last time you worked overtime?

How many hours do you usually work overtime?

How many hours was your longest overtime?

Should companies be able to force employees to work overtime?

Should companies be forced to pay employees for any overtime they work?

15. BUSINESS TRIPS

What are the advantages and disadvantages of frequent business travel?

Would you like to travel as part of your job?

How often do you go on business trips?

When and where was your last business trip?

What is your most memorable business trip?

Which country would you most like to visit in your next business trip?

Which country would you least like to visit again in your next business trip?

How do you feel about business trips?

Why are business trips important?

16. EXPERIENCE

How long have you been in your current company?

How long do you plan to stay with your current company?

How long did you stay with your first company?

In your country, how common is it to stay with a company for a long time?

What professional experience has been the most important in your career so far? Why?

17. PROMOTION & DEMOTION

When was your last promotion?

When are you expecting to get a promotion?

How old is your oldest co-worker?

How young is your youngest co-worker?

How important is getting a promotion to you?

What is the best way to be promoted?

How can office politics affect promotion?

What would be your reaction if you got promoted tomorrow?

How common is demotion in your company?

Why would someone get demoted?

18. PROBATIONARY PERIOD

How long is your company's probationary period?

How long did it take for you to get a permanent position?

What are the differences between a regular employee and someone on probation?

Are there any ways for someone to be made permanent faster? What are they?

19. CONTRACTS

How many workers do you have in your company?

How common are permanent contracts in your country?

How do you feel about the general way companies contract workers in your country?

Who benefits more from contracts, the worker or the company?

Would you consider working under a third-party agency?

Why do people consider working under third party agencies?

Why do companies hire from third party agencies?

What are the benefits of hiring workers from third party agencies?

If you were a business owner, would you consider hiring workers from third party agencies? Why?

How long should an employee be under probation?

20. WORK-LIFE BALANCE

In your own words, how would you define work-life balance?

How important is work-life balance? Why?

Who benefits from work-life balance?

How can you achieve work-life balance in your life?

How much work-life balance do you currently have?

What initiatives does your company have with regards to work-life balance?

How can the government help in achieving work-life balance for workers in your country or region?

Describe someone you know who has a great work-life balance.

For you, what activities help in achieving work-life balance?

21. MANAGEMENT & LEADERSHIP

What are the advantages of being a boss?

What are the disadvantages of being a boss?

What are some qualities of a good boss?

What are some qualities of a bad boss?

Who is the best boss you've ever had?

How often do you talk to your boss?

How often does your boss check on you?

How often does your boss hangout with your team?

What are the traits you like most about your current boss?

How common is it in your country for employees to address their bosses with sir/ma'am?

If you were given a choice, would you like to be given more management responsibilies? Why?

What does your boss say when you come in late for work?

In your own words, how would you define a leader?

Is there a difference between a manager and a leader? Why?

Is it necessary to be a good leader in order to be a good manager?

22. BEING AN EMPLOYEE

What was your very first job?

When did you land your first job?

What are the advantages of being a normal employee and not having any people management duties?

What are the disadvantages of being a normal employee and not having any people management duties?

Would you like to have one job for your whole life with a good, steady salary or do you need change to stay motivated?

23. FREELANCING

How common is freelancing in your country?

Why do some people choose to work as freelancers?

What are the advantages of working as a freelancer?

What are the disadvantages of working as a freelancer?

What is the best thing about being a freelancer?

What is the worst thing about working as a freelancer?

If you were given a chance, would you work as a freelancer? Why?

What are the most common jobs of freelancers?

24. DIFFERENT PROFESSIONS

What are some examples of professions that suit your personality?

What is the worst job you can think of for your personality?

What are the most prestigious professions in your country? Why?

Who do you think should be the most well paid in terms of jobs?

Who do you think should be the least paid in terms of jobs?

What was your dream job when you were a kid?

What is your dream job now?

Given the opportunity, would you pursue your dream job? Why or why not?

How well paid are politicians in your country?

What is the most in demand job in your country?

25. JOB REQUIREMENTS

How important is educational achievement when applying for a job in your country?

Which is more important, qualifications or experience? Why?

How important is experience when applying for a job in your country?

In your country, how challenging is it to find a job for newly graduated candidates?

Was it difficult to get your first job?

What assistance do recent graduates get from the government when applying for jobs?

26. JOB INTERVIEWS

How was your first ever interview? Describe your experience. What did you do well and what did you do badly?

How do you feel during interviews?

How do you prepare before your interviews?

What clothes do you wear in interviews?

How important are first impressions in interviews?

What makes you stand out from other applicants when you apply for a job? (What are your strong points?)

What's your biggest weakness?

How do you see your career evolving in the next 2 years?

Do you think job interviews are a fair assessment of a candidate's suitability for a job?

If you were an interviewer, what you look for in an applicant?

27. BENEFITS & PERKS

What do you look for in a company?

Rank the following benefits and perks in order of importance for you. Explain your answers:

- Frequent travel
- Management responsibilities
- Child-care benefits
- Long holidays
- Travel and food allowances
- Frequent social events and activities organized by the company
- The option to work from home

What benefits and perks would you most like to have in your current position?

28. RESIGNATION

What is the most common reason for someone to resign?

What was the reason why you left your previous job?

What's the difference between termination and resignation?

Would you ever consider leaving your current position? What would it take for you to leave?

How would you feel if your closest co-worker resigned?

How would you feel if your current boss resigned?

How do you think your co-workers would feel if you resigned?

How do you think your boss would feel if you resigned?

29. JOB-HOPPING

How many jobs have you had in the past five years?

How common is it for people to change jobs in your country?

What do you think about job-hopping?

Why do some people job-hop?

How can job-hopping affect your career?

30. SALARY

How do you feel about your first ever salary?

What is your ideal salary? Why?

How important is salary in applying for a job?

What is the common salary range for your chosen profession?

How important are salary increases for staff motivation?

Is salary the most important factor in a job?

Would you rather do something you love for a low salary or something you hate for a high salary? Why?

Is it good for governments to introduce laws to guarantee a minimum wage? Why or why not?

31. CHOOSING A COMPANY

What are the factors you consider when choosing a company?

How do you find job openings?

What is the most effective way of finding jobs?

How important is company image in choosing a company?

How important is location when choosing a company?

How important is personal growth when choosing a company?

How important is professional growth when choosing a company?

How important is diversity when choosing a company?

32. FEELINGS ABOUT YOUR JOB

How much do you like your job? (Be as sincere as possible 🙂)

Why do you (or don't you) like your job?

What is your favorite part about your job?

33. OFFICEMATES/CO-WORKERS

What kind of people do you like to work with?

What kind of people are you working with now?

Who do you prefer working with, young or old employees?

Who do you prefer working with, male or female employees?

Would you consider yourself a workaholic? Why?

Would you consider yourself easy going? Why?

What do you think about people who are easy going in their jobs?

34. RETIREMENT

When do you plan to retire?

Why do you think some people never want to retire and others can't wait to retire?

What is your ideal retirement?

At what age do people in your country usually retire?

Where would you like to spend your retirement?

35. EMAIL

How many emails do you receive in a day?

How helpful is emailing in your job?

Why is it sometimes easier to have misunderstandings with people during email exchanges?

Do you sometimes feel overwhelmed by the number of emails in your inbox? Do you have any tricks to tackle this problem?

What are the advantages and disadvantages of using office memos to communicate with staff?

36. MEETINGS

How do you feel about meetings?

When was the last time you attended a meeting?

What do you think about lunch meetings?

Which do you prefer, formal or informal meetings? Why?

Have you ever 'dozed off' while in a meeting?

When was the last time you dozed off in a meeting?

Do you prefer traditional meetings or teleconferences?

37. CONFERENCES

How many conferences do you have in a year?

How do you feel about conferences?

Describe the last conference you attended.

38. TECHNOLOGY

How often do you answer phone calls in your current job?

How often do you use your cellphone at work?

What kind of technology do you use at the office?

How has technology changed the way we work?

How has technology changed the way we learn?

39. OFFICE ENVIRONMENT

How would you describe your current office environment?

How important is office environment?

What is your ideal work environment?

How many co-workers can you count as friends?

How do you feel about office politics?

How rampant is office politics in your company?

** BONUS SPEAKING CARDS SECTION **

40. MEDIA

If you could keep only one form of media, which would you choose?	Is there such a thing as an unbiased source of news?
Radio is over a hundred years old. Why hasn't it ever been replaced by a more modern form of media?	What would happen if the media just stopped?
How influenced are you by the media?	How can students use different parts of the media to improve their language skills?
Should the government control the press?	Are newspapers becoming obsolete?

41. HOTELS

Would you like to work in a hotel?	What are the advantages and disadvantages of staying in a hotel?
Do you use the spa and leisure facilities when you stay at a hotel?	If you were the manager of an old two-star hotel that was in danger of closure, how would you try to make it profitable again?
How would you describe a typical day's work of a hotel receptionist?	What is your opinion of large, all-inclusive resort hotels?
Do you think it is acceptable to take things such as bathrobes, soap, etc, from a hotel room when you leave?	Does your behaviour differ when staying in a hotel compared to when you are at home?

42. LANGUAGES

What are the advantages and disadvantages of English becoming a global language?	Which language do you think would be the best global language?
What body language do you use in your culture?	Is preserving a dying language as important as preserving an endangered species?
Apart from English, which other language would you like to learn?	Do you agree that English is essential for success in one's career?
What age is the best to start learning a new language?	What is more important when speaking a foreign language: fluency or accuracy?

43. TECHNOLOGY

Has technology made our lives more complicated?	Do technological advances increase the gap between rich and poor?
Which areas of technology are the most important to teach at school?	Which invention has had a more positive impact on our lives: the mobile phone or personal computer?
Do you agree that technology has made us lazy?	Do you believe that advances in technology causes job losses?
If mobile phones disappeared one day, how do you think people would cope?	In your opinion, which industry has been most transformed by technology?

44. ART

How would you describe your relationship with art?	What paintings, drawings, or sculptures do you have in your home?
Is collecting works of art a good investment?	What's the point in owning a valuable piece of art if it has to be kept locked away?
Do you go to art exhibitions, galleries, antique markets?	What is your definition of art?
Who is the most famous artist from your country?	Is there any public art in your city?

45. HISTORY

Do you think it is important to have a knowledge of history?	What period of history would you like to learn more about?
Should history lessons focus on politics and war, or on social changes?	Which local historical figure has had the greatest impact on your country?
What do you think of the recent history of your country, the past 30 years?	Which historical figure would you like to meet?
Do you think history repeats itself?	Are you proud of the history of your country?

46. BOOKS

How important is reading books?	What should be the roles of libraries in modern life?
If you could write a book, what kind of book (genre) would it be?	Would you go to bookshops more often if they were friendly places with comfortable armchairs and coffee shops?
Could you live in a world without books?	What is the worst book that you've ever read?
Have you read more than one book by the same author?	How can we encourage children to read more?

Speaking Phrases (Student Handout)

Likes/dislikes	Opinion
I'm into... I'm a keen/avid (surfer) I'm keen on/fond of (surfing) I (go surfing) to unwind, to escape the stresses and strains of my day to day life. I like nothing more than (to go surfing) I'm itching to try/go.... (I really want to)	As far as I'm concerned, As I see it, From my point of view, In my humble opinion, I'd say that...
Comparing/contrasting Both pictures show... In this picture they look as though they are.... Whereas/while in this picture... In contrast On the other hand	**Describing pictures** The first thing that strikes me about this picture is... The thing that really jumps out of this picture is... In this picture it looks as if/though they are... They could/might/may be... They could/might/may have just... I'm pretty sure that they're feeling... I'd guess that they are...
Agreeing We see eye to eye. Yeah, I'd go along with that. Absolutely! You took the words right out of my mouth. I couldn't agree more.	**Disagreeing** We don't see eye to eye. I take your point but... I tend to disagree with you there. That's not always the case

You have a point there. I'm with you 100% on this one.	I beg to differ Isn't it more a case of…
Starting to make a conclusion Let's get down to the nitty gritty. The bottom line is we have to choose one… It's a tough one, I'm torn between … and …. Shall we go with ….?	**Asking for opinion** What's your take on….? Where do you stand on….? In my opinion…., would you go along with that? What are your thoughts on this?
Personalising Speaking from personal experience,… For me personally,.. This is a topic that is particularly close to my heart… It's funny I was just thinking about this the other day. My gut/initial reaction is… If I were to choose one of these situations (part 2 pictures), I'd go with… because…	**Impressive structures** Another point I'd like to add about … is… It's also worth bearing in mind that… Coming back to what (Javi) was saying about …. I'd also like to point out that… I think it's important not to forget that… The vast majority of people tend to think that… At the end of the day… When all's said and done…
Tips Eye-contact Active listening Open body language Speak up Don't dominate	**Asking for repetition** I beg your pardon, I didn't catch that. Sorry would you mind repeating that? Could you repeat the question please?

Student Handout: How to Learn Thousands of Words in English in Only 6 Months

Do you spend a lot of time and effort in learning vocabulary but still find difficulty using it when required? Have you spent a lot of time memorizing vocabulary words but forget them when you need them the most? Don't worry if you answered a big resounding "YES" to any of these questions because you are not alone. There are a number of useful tools, methods, and exercises which will have you not only remembering, but using your extended vocabulary with minimal effort. Let's get started!

Use Mnemonic Devices

What are mnemonic devices? Well they include a variety of techniques and methods that help remember or recall information.

FANBOYS

For example, many students often need to recall the conjunctions used in English grammar. Remembering FANBOYS is a good tool to recall these words (For, And, Nor, But, Or, Yet, So). The best part of this is you can use your creativity to make it interesting and different. You could create a song out of the words, similar to what many children do when they learn names of countries and capitals. Finding some words that rhyme together would give your song some rhythm, so get creative and don't be afraid to try something a bit silly. Silly is good because it helps the brain remember.

Tongue twisters

Tongue twisters are a fun way of practicing sounds, and this repetition of sounds creates another type of rhythm: *Silly Sally sat by the seashore collecting seashells.*

This can be done with words that begin with the same sound or even have similar sounds within or at the end of a word. It can create an interesting beat or jingle which helps you remember easily and quickly.

Teach it to the mirror!

One of the best and easiest ways to remember anything is to teach someone else. If you can't teach someone else, then teach yourself in the mirror!

Share your knowledge. In order to teach vocabulary to someone else, you need to have a good grasp of the word and the many contexts in which it is used. In fact, if you refer to a dictionary you may find that there are multiple definitions related to the word itself. Before teaching, it's important to study and thoroughly understand the word first. Look for sentences that contain that word so you can understand how it can be used with other words for meaning. Practice making your own sentences as well. Encourage the "student" to ask questions for understanding and clarity.

Make it a part of your daily routine

Now it's important to use what you have learned. As the saying goes: "If you don't use it, you lose it." The first step here is to look for ways to use the new words.

Notecards or post-it notes

Notecards or post-it notes are useful as they are handy. You can stick post-its anywhere as a reminder. Just write the name, short definition, or even a sentence as an example. Here's what your notecard could look like:

Impart: to make known

Synonyms: tell, disclose

Sentence: Teachers impart knowledge to their students.

Learn Suffixes

Suffixes are word endings that may change a word's meaning. They can be used to change a word so that it maintains the rules of grammar. Consider the following sentences

It is a tradition in Chinese culture to eat using chopsticks.

The older generation is more traditional than today's youth.

The wedding ceremony is traditionally conducted by a priest.

Learning suffixes and how they change words is a useful tool. With the suffix -ally, as in "traditionally", it is understood that we are using an adverb describing an action. The –tion in "tradition" makes it a noun, so it's often placed at the beginning of a sentence. Understanding placement of words will help you make sure sentences are grammatically correct.

Read, Read, and Read!

Today's fast paced lifestyle makes it challenging, if not impossible, to make the time to read. However, tor increasing English vocabulary, it's absolutely essential. Read what you enjoy reading in your own language but read it in English! If you like music, read about music, if you like business, read business!

The 30-minute Rule

The 30-minute Rule states that thirty minutes of pleasurable reading every day will lead to amazing results in your level of English over time. 'Thirty-minute readers', people who read for fun for at least 30 minutes per day, tend to have a vast vocabulary. Furthermore, several studies have suggested that the health benefits can be considerable: living longer, increasing IQ, and reducing stress among other perks. Over time, reading regularly can also increase vocabulary and make it easier to utilize these words in practical and functional situations.

Don't worry if you can't find the time in a busy lifestyle to pick up a book to read.

Look for friends or colleagues who enjoy reading. Often times, interacting with bookworms or avid readers will help you pick up vocabulary or new expressions from them. Don't hesitate to ask about anything that is unfamiliar.

Read Newspapers

A newspaper is a very valuable tool that has a wealth of information at your fingertips. Whether it's the paper version or the electronic version, it doesn't matter. Newspapers are a tool which will spark curiosity and encourage you to read more about a variety of topics.

Spend time interacting with expert professionals in various fields if you can.

That doesn't mean you need to spend time at colleges or universities. Expand your field of awareness and interest to connect to those outside your circle of friends and colleagues. You can join various chat forums or groups in social media. Learn new vocabulary and subjects. You will definitely see the difference.

Download a dictionary app

Anyone who wants to improve their vocabulary really must download an app to their phone. It's not at all practical to lug around a dictionary. A dictionary app on a smartphone can be accessed quickly. Also, being familiar with some online tools that give sentence examples using the words in different contexts is extremely useful. Remember that words fit together in sentences based on their meaning, so it's important to always understand the context or surrounding words so that the sentence or expression makes sense.

Record sentences and structures in your notebook, never single words

NEVER write a single word followed by a definition in your notebook! Always add an example sentence and pay attention to the original sentence where you saw this word. English words can often change meanings depending on the prepositions they go with or the type of sentence they are in.

For example:

He was turned away at the door because he was wearing trainers.

Meaning: He was rejected

He turned away when I tried to speak to him because he was very angry.

Meaning: He looked the other way or turned his head towards a different direction so he didn't have to look at me.

Make it fun!

Learning new English vocabulary words doesn't have to be a chore! Find ways to make it fun, interesting, and rewarding. Download a few gaming apps that focus on building or using vocabulary words. A common one is "Words with Friends" where you get to share and learn new words with your own circle of friends. Try it! You will see the results.

SIGN UP TO MY NEWSLETTER FOR A FREE BOOK AND TONS OF FREE RESOURCES & GOODIES!

https://www.idmadrid.es/vip-resources

ONE LAST THING...

If you enjoyed this book or found it useful I'd be very grateful if you'd post a short review on Amazon. Your support really does make a difference and I read all the reviews personally so I can get your feedback and make this book even better.

If you'd like to leave a review then all you need to do is click the review link on this book's page on Amazon.

Thanks for reading and thanks again for your support!

Made in the USA
Columbia, SC
04 June 2025